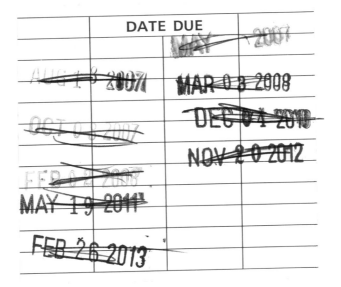

| | DATE DUE | |
|---|---|---|
| | ~~MAY 2007~~ | |
| ~~AUG 1 2 2007~~ | ~~MAR 0 3 2008~~ | |
| ~~OCT 0 2007~~ | ~~DEC 04 2010~~ | |
| ~~FEB 0 2008~~ | ~~NOV 2 0 2012~~ | |
| ~~MAY 1 9 2011~~ | | |
| ~~FEB 26 2013~~ | | |

# President
# George
# Washington

by DAVID A. ADLER

illustrated by

JOHN WALLNER

Holiday House / New York

To Rivkah, Eliyahu, and Sarah
D. A. A.

To my dad and to the enduring American spirit
J. W.

Text copyright © 2005 by David A. Adler
Illustrations copyright © 2005 by John C. Wallner
All Rights Reserved
Printed in the United States of America
Reading Level: 2.9
www.holidayhouse.com
First Edition
1 3 5 7 9 10 8 6 4 2

Library of Congress Cataloging-in-Publication Data
Adler, David A.
President George Washington / by David A. Adler;
illustrated by John Wallner.— 1st ed.
p. cm.
ISBN 0-8234-1604-6 (hardcover)
1. Washington, George, 1732–1799—Juvenile literature.
2. Presidents—United States—Biography—Juvenile literature.
[1. Washington, George, 1732–1799. 2. Presidents.]
I. Wallner, John C., ill. II. Title.

E312.66 .A38 2001
973.4'1'092—dc21
[B]   00-039607

# Contents

# 1. Young George Washington

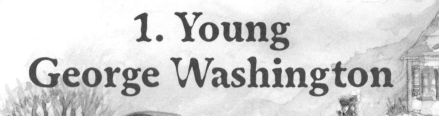

George Washington was born
on February 22, 1732.
He was born in a small
Virginia farmhouse.
Virginia was an English colony.
The people were loyal
to King George II of England.

The Washingtons grew tobacco,
fruit, and vegetables on their farm.
Most of the work was done
by African-American slaves.

When George was seven,
he learned to read and write.
He liked to write.
He copied from a book of rules.
"Keep your fingers clean," he wrote.

"Kill no vermin, fleas, lice or ticks
in the sight of others."
George studied arithmetic too.
It was his favorite subject.

He also liked to fish, swim, and hunt.
Most of all,
he loved to ride his horse.

When George was eleven,
his father died.
Now George needed
to help his mother on the farm.
He also helped her
with his younger sister, Elizabeth,
and younger brothers,
Samuel, John Augustine, and Charles.

When George was fourteen,

he wanted to go to sea.

But his mother wouldn't let him go.

So George became a surveyor.

He went into the woods.

He marked out the land for new farms.

In 1751, George Washington
was nineteen.
He joined the Virginia army.
He was a soldier.

# 2. George Washington and Martha Custis

The English and the French
wanted the Ohio Valley.
George Washington was sent there.
He told the French
to get off English land.
The French said no.
A few months later,
George Washington was back
in the Ohio Valley.

This time he came
with a troop of soldiers.
They fought the French
and beat them.
It was Washington's first battle.
It was the start
of the French and Indian War.

"I have heard the bullets whistle,"
Washington wrote in a letter.
"There is something charming
in the sound."
Washington was in other battles.
Bullets tore through his jacket
and hat.
But George Washington
was never hurt.
Soon he was an American hero.
In 1758 he left the army.
He went home to Virginia
and met Martha Custis.

Martha was a rich, young widow.
She had two children.
"I'm an old fashioned housekeeper,"
she said of herself,
"busy as a bee, steady as a clock,
and cheerful as a cricket."
George Washington and
Martha Custis married
on January 6, 1759.
George called Martha "Patsy."
Martha called George
"My Old Man."

# 3. Taxes and Protests

The French and Indian War
ended in 1763.
The English won.
But the war was costly.
The new king, King George III,
wanted Americans
to help pay for the war.
He taxed them
and they protested.

In 1773, to protest the tax on tea,
some Americans
dumped 342 chests of tea
into Boston Harbor.
By April 1775
the thirteen American colonies
were at war with the English.
They wanted to be free
of English rule.

In May 1775
leaders of the colonies met.
They talked about their fight
with the English.
George Washington was there.

George Washington
wore his old army uniform.
His uniform told everyone
he was ready to fight.
The leaders chose him
to lead the fight against England.

# 4. President
# George Washington

Sometimes there was not enough food
or money to pay Washington's men.
There were not enough
uniforms or guns.
Sometimes the men would not
follow Washington's orders.

"I have often thought,"
   Washington wrote in a letter,
"how much happier
   I should have been,
   if, instead of accepting a command . . .
   I had taken my musket
   upon my shoulders"
   and was just one of the soldiers.

Washington's army won battles
in Boston and Trenton.
The English won battles
in New York and Philadelphia.
In 1778 the French
joined the fight against England.
There were other battles, too.
Many people died.

In September 1781,
the Americans and the French
fought the English
in Yorktown, Virginia.
It was the last big battle
of the Revolutionary War.

The Americans and the French
beat the English.
The Americans would be free
of English rule.

In September 1783
the Americans and the English
agreed to end the fighting.
A nation was born.
The thirteen colonies
became the first thirteen states
of the United States of America.
In 1789 George Washington
was elected the first president
of the United States.

President Washington
kept the new nation at peace.
He led it for eight years
until 1797.
Then he went home to Virginia.

# 5. First in the Hearts

In December 1799,
George Washington became ill.
By the afternoon of December 14
he said, "I find I am going."
Martha was with him.
"I die hard," Washington said,
"but I am not afraid to go."
He died that night.

Martha Washington said,
"I shall soon follow him."
She died on May 22, 1802.
People everywhere
mourned the death
of George Washington.

It was said that
George Washington was
"first in war,
first in peace,
and first in the hearts
of his fellow-citizens."

# Important Dates

**February 22, 1732**

George Washington is born in Virginia.

**April 12, 1743**

His father, Augustine Washington, dies.

**1751**

George Washington joins the Virginia army.

**January 6, 1759**

George Washington marries Martha Custis.

**1775–1783**

Washington is commander in chief of the Continental army.

**1789–1797**

He serves as the first president of the United States.

**December 14, 1799**

George Washington dies.

# Suggested Reading

Armentrout, David. *George Washington*. Vero Beach, Fla.: Rourke Publishing, 2003.

Burke, Rick. *George Washington*. Chicago: Heinemann Library, 2002.

Mara, Wil. *George Washington*. New York: Children's Press, 2002.

Nettleton, Pamela Hill. *George Washington: Farmer, Soldier, President*. Minneapolis: Picture Window Books, 2003.

# Notes

Chapter 1: I found the "Keep your fingers" quote in the Seelye biography (p. 14).

Chapter 2: I found the "I have heard the bullets whistle" quote in the Wilson biography (p. 77) and the "busy as a bee" quote in the McConnell book (p. 14).

Chapter 4: The "how much happier I should have been" quote is from the Hughes biography (volume II, p. 336).

Chapter 5: The quotes "I die hard" and "I shall soon follow him" are from Lossing's book (pp. 334, 336). I found John Marshall's quote, "first in war" in Irving's biography (vol. II, p. 499–500).

# Sources

Emery, Noemie. *Washington: A Biography*. New York: G. P. Putnam's Sons, 1976.

Flexner, James Thomas. *Washington: The Indispensable Man*. Boston: Little, Brown, 1974.

Freeman, Douglas Southall. *George Washington*. New York: Charles Scribner's Sons, 1954.

Hughes, Rupert. *George Washington*. New York: William Morrow, 1927.

Irving, Washington. *Life of George Washington*. New York: G. Putnam Broadway, 1855–1859.

Lossing, Benson J. *The Home of Washington*. Hartford, Conn.: A. S. Hale, 1870.

McConnell, Jane, and Burt McConnell. *Our First Ladies*. New York: Thomas Y. Crowell, 1964.

Seelye, Elizabeth Eggleston. *The Story of Washington*. New York: D. Appleton and Company, 1893.

Wilson, Woodrow. *George Washington*. New York: Harper & Brothers, 1898.